BASIC BIOLOGY

Green Plants

DENISE WALKER

A+

Smart Apple Media

First published in 2006 by Evans Brothers Ltd.
2A Portman Mansions, Chiltern Street,
London W1U 6NR

Series editor: Harriet Brown, Editor: Harriet
Brown, Design: Simon Morse, Illustrations:
Ian Thompson

Published in the United States by
Smart Apple Media
2140 Howard Drive West, North Mankato,
Minnesota 56003

Library of Congress Cataloging-in-
Publication Data

Walker, Denise.
Green plants / by Denise Walker.
p. cm. — (Basic biology)
Includes index.
ISBN-13: 978-1-58340-993-0
1. Plant physiology. 2. Plants—Nutrition.
3. Plants—Assimilation. I. Title.

QK711.2.W35 2006
571.2—dc22   2006002523

9 8 7 6 5 4 3 2 1

Contents

Introduction

Green plants are all around us—from microscopic algae to enormous trees, from spiky cacti to brightly colored flowering plants. Plant species have successfully adapted so that they are able to occupy almost every environment on Earth.

This book takes you on a journey to discover more about the wonderful world of green plants. Find out what green plants need to thrive and grow, discover what happens if their requirements are not fulfilled, and learn about how they contribute to the environments in which they live.

Discover how plants gain energy from the sun, how they photosynthesize, respire, and reproduce. Learn all about how plants spread their seeds in an attempt to make sure their offspring survive, and find out how some plants can even reproduce without seeds. Read about how man relies on plants and how their absence would spell disaster for life on our planet.

This book contains feature boxes that will help you unravel more about the mysteries of green plants. Test yourself on what you have learned so far, investigate some of the concepts discussed, find out more key facts, and discover some of the scientific findings of the past and how these might be utilized in the future.

Did you know?

▶ Look for these boxes—they contain surprising and fascinating facts about green plants.

Test yourself

▶ Use these boxes to see how much you've learned. Try to answer the questions without looking at the book, but take a look if you are really stuck.

Investigate

▶ These boxes contain experiments you can carry out at home. The equipment you will need is usually cheap and easy to find.

Time travel

These boxes contain scientific discoveries from the past and fascinating developments that pave the way for the advance of science in the future.

Answers

At the end of this book, on pages 46 and 47, you will find the answers to the questions from the "Test yourself" and "Investigate" boxes.

Glossary

Words highlighted in **bold** are described in detail in the glossary on pages 46 and 47.

Plants and their requirements

Green plants are the basis of all life on Earth. Green plants do not rely on other organisms to provide them with food. Instead, they use the sun's energy to make their own food in a process called **photosynthesis**. During photosynthesis, plants take in carbon dioxide and produce oxygen. Oxygen is essential for the survival of humans and other animals. Green plants are also the basis of most **food chains,** and many other organisms rely on them for their own survival. Any threat to green plants is a threat to life on Earth. Through dependence on green plants, nearly all living things depend on energy from the sun.

WHAT DO PLANTS NEED TO STAY HEALTHY?

Look at the first photograph. This is obviously a healthy tree, but can you explain why? The tree looks healthy because it has many green leaves. It is not wilting or drooping and looks as though it will survive for some time. Another sign of a healthy plant is the presence of blossoms or fruit, which would indicate that reproduction is taking place.

Now consider the second photograph. This tree looks unhealthy, but why? Its leaves are brown and shriveled, even though it is an evergreen tree, and there is no sign of any new growth, blossoms, or seeds. In nonwoody plants, another sign of an unhealthy plant is a wilting or drooping stem.

Why do these trees look so different? Plants need sunlight, water, carbon dioxide, and mineral nutrients for survival. The healthy tree has received all of these ingredients, whereas the unhealthy tree is lacking in one or more of these ingredients.

▲ This tree is covered with leaves, which indicate that it is growing and healthy.

This tree is lacking one or more of its essential requirements. Its soil may not have enough nutrients, or fresh water may be in short supply.

CARBON DIOXIDE

Plants take in carbon dioxide through their leaves. During photosynthesis, carbon dioxide reacts with water to produce oxygen and glucose. Glucose is the plant's food. It is stored in the leaves as starch until the plant needs energy.

SUNLIGHT

Plants need sunlight as their source of energy. When sunlight is present, plants manufacture their own food through the process of photosynthesis. When sunlight is not present, they convert the food they have made to energy by the process of **respiration** (see page 30).

WATER

Plants use water for support. Water keeps the stems and leaves firm. Plants that do not have enough water will wilt and droop. Mineral nutrients are dissolved in the water found in soil. When water enters a plant's roots, the plant gains essential mineral nutrients, such as nitrogen and phosphorus.

OXYGEN

Oxygen is not necessary for photosynthesis; instead, it is a by-product of photosynthesis. However, at times when plants cannot photosynthesize, they switch to the process of respiration. During respiration, plants use oxygen to release the energy from their food.

MINERAL NUTRIENTS

Even when green plants have a plentiful supply of sunlight, carbon dioxide, and water, they may not always be healthy. Plant cells contain protein. Protein contains nitrogen. To maintain their cells, plants need a source of nitrogen, which comes from mineral nutrients. Other mineral nutrients are also essential to a plant's survival. Scientists have carried out water culture experiments to find out which mineral nutrients plants need.

▲ To grow a healthy crop, the conditions must be correct. If any one of a crop's requirements are lacking, it will not flourish.

DID YOU KNOW?

▶ A British chemist decided to spend two weeks in a sealed chamber to see whether a crop of wheat plants could supply all of his oxygen needs. The chamber was 10 feet (3 m) long and 10 feet (3 m) wide. A connecting room held 30,000 wheat plants, which gave off an average of 5 pounds (2.3 kg) of oxygen each day. The plants supplied more than enough oxygen for the man to survive, but the amount of carbon dioxide he gave off in return was not sufficient for plant survival— more had to be pumped in! The experiment clearly shows the close relationship we have with green plants

TEST YOURSELF

▶ For each of the following plants, think about and then explain how it obtains its requirements for photosynthesis.
(1) A cactus in a dry desert.
(2) A water lily on a pond.

WATER CULTURE EXPERIMENTS

Fast-growing seedlings (very young plants) are grown in a solution of distilled water in which certain mineral nutrients are dissolved. To find out what happens when one mineral nutrient is lacking, it is left out of the culture solution. While the seedlings grow, scientists observe the effect of the mineral nutrient's absence. To draw firm conclusions from the experiment, many seedlings are grown, and the experiment is repeated several times.

WHICH MINERAL NUTRIENTS DO PLANTS NEED?

Minerals left out of culture solution	Effect on plant
Nitrates	Poor growth. Proteins not made. Yellowing of the leaves.
Sulfates	Excessive root growth. Proteins not made. Yellowing of young leaves.
Phosphates	Poor plant growth.
Potassium	Poor plant growth. Water lost. Yellowing and abnormal leaf shape.
Calcium	Abnormal leaf shape, stunted plants, and poor growth.
Magnesium	Yellowing of older leaves. No **chlorophyll** (see page 20).
Iron	Yellowing of young leaves. No chlorophyll.

TEST YOURSELF

▶ The following water culture experiments were set up:

(1) Seedling grown in the absence of calcium.
(2) Seedling grown in the absence of phosphates.
(3) Seedling grown in the absence of nitrates.
(4) Seedling grown in a solution containing all necessary mineral nutrients.
(5) Seedling grown in pure distilled water without the addition of any mineral nutrients.

The experiment was left for six weeks. During this time, what factors do you think should be kept the same and why? How could changes in the seedlings be measured? Describe the effects of the experiment on each seedling.

FERTILE AND INFERTILE SOIL

Soil that has a good supply of mineral nutrients is called fertile soil. Soil lacking in essential mineral nutrients is called infertile soil. In a natural, unmanaged woodland or field, plants use up soil nutrients. When a plant dies, it **decomposes** (breaks down), and the nutrients are returned to the soil. Plant crops grown by farmers are harvested each year, and no nutrients are returned to the soil. When this happens year after year, the soil nutrients are depleted. So, when soil does not contain sufficient nutrients, farmers and gardeners may apply a fertilizer.

ARTIFICIAL FERTILIZERS

Artificial fertilizers are chemicals that have been manufactured to improve plant growth. When they are used, the yield of a crop will increase. Artificial fertilizers are usually water-soluble and are sprayed onto the soil or onto the crop in a watery solution. This has two main advantages: (1) By mixing the fertilizer with water, it is used in a more economical way, so less fertilizer is needed. (2) The fertilizer can pass easily into the plant through the roots or through the leaves.

The most common artificial fertilizers are called NPK fertilizers. These letters are the chemical symbols for the three main ingredients. N is nitrogen, P is phosphorus, and K is potassium. Since phosphorus and potassium are too reactive on their own, fertilizer manufacturers use chemical processes to convert them into other substances called phosphates and salts of potassium. Fertilizers are manufactured to a specific concentration, depending on the crops for which they are intended.

▶ This soil has not received natural nutrients as a result of plant breakdown or any artificial or natural fertilizer. It cannot easily support any plant growth.

▲ In a deciduous woodland, leaves fall to the floor each autumn. These break down and release nutrients, which return to the soil.

NATURAL FERTILIZERS

Organic farming relies on the use of natural fertilizers rather than artificial fertilizers. Natural fertilizers include manure and dung, fish meal, dried blood, compost, sewage sludge, and crop leftovers. Most natural fertilizers add structure to the soil because they contain a substance called humus. Humus is made from dead plant material. It prevents the soil from blowing away in the wind or being washed away by rain. It holds the equivalent of 80 to 90 percent of its own weight as moisture and is often described as the "life force" of soil.

▲ These organically grown vegetables are relatively small compared with those grown using artificial fertilizers.

▲ This humus is extremely valuable to gardeners and farmers because it promotes healthy soil that can support plant life.

Natural fertilizers are much cheaper than their chemical equivalent. However, natural fertilizers also have their disadvantages. It is more difficult to spread natural fertilizers, they can smell very bad, the release of nutrients is relatively slow, and their

use results in smaller crops compared with the use of artificial fertilizers. In addition, the exact amount of each nutrient is not known, and the farmer cannot apply it accordingly.

Natural fertilizers are commonly used by businesses where the crop areas are relatively small and therefore easier to treat. It is more expensive to produce, for example, 10 pounds (4.5 kg) of organic carrots than it is to produce 10 pounds (4.5 kg) of nonorganic carrots. This is because each organic carrot is usually smaller than each nonorganic carrot, and the yields are not as high. Therefore, organic produce tends to be more expensive to buy than nonorganic produce. However, some customers prefer products that have not been exposed to chemical fertilizers and pesticides (chemicals used to kill pests such as some insects).

In some parts of the world, human excrement is used as fertilizer. When it is raw and untreated, it is called "night soil." It is nutrient-rich and helps improve soil fertility and plant yields. However, there are problems associated with its use, and it is illegal in some countries. If the excrement is not properly treated, it can be dangerous to use. It may contain disease-carrying microorganisms, and there have been cases of disease-carrying vegetables. One traditional way of avoiding the dangers of night soil in places such as China is by not eating raw foods.

To treat night soil so that it is safe to use on crops, it must be composted. This means that it should be left to decompose at temperatures above 113 °F (45 °C). It should be left for a certain length of time so that biological activity has killed most of the dangerous microorganisms. It must then be allowed to cure at temperatures between 68 and 104 °F (40 °C) until all toxins are removed. Once it is ready for safe use on crops, it is called humanure.

Seaweed is plentiful in some coastal areas of the world. It is inexpensive and rich in nutrients, which makes it an excellent fertilizer. Farms in Scotland in the United Kingdom (UK) have traditionally used seaweed to fertilize oat crops. It is dug directly into the soil.

INVESTIGATE

▶ Use library books and the Internet to research the differences between organic and nonorganic farming. Design a brochure to help people understand the differences.

▼ Where seaweed is abundant, such as on the Scottish coast, its use as a fertilizer is an important source of nutrients.

The nitrogen cycle

All life-forms, including plants, require nitrogen. Without nitrogen, a plant cannot make proteins, including **enzymes** (proteins that speed up biochemical reactions). Plants get their nitrogen from the soil, but how does it get there in the first place? The majority of Earth's atmosphere is nitrogen, but most organisms cannot use it in this form. Plants need nitrogen in its "fixed" (combined) form, as part of a **compound** such as nitrate ions, ammonia, or urea. Nitrogen undergoes a cycle— atmospheric nitrogen enters the soil, becomes part of a plant or animal, and is eventually returned to the environment to begin the cycle all over again.

THE NITROGEN CYCLE

Nitrogen undergoes its cycle from the air to the ground; to animals, plants, and bacteria; and back to the air, constantly.

THE ATMOSPHERE

The air contains 79 percent nitrogen. The massive amount of energy in lightning breaks down nitrogen **molecules** in the air into nitrogen **atoms**. They combine with oxygen to form nitrogen oxides. When nitrogen oxides dissolve in rain, they form nitrates. The nitrates fall to the ground in the rain. This is called atmospheric fixation.

NITROGEN-FIXING BACTERIA

Nitrogen-fixing means taking nitrogen from the air and combining it with other chemicals, which turns it into a compound. Most nitrogen-fixing organisms are bacteria. They are found independently in the soil or in close association with a specific plant. For example, the root nodules of legumes (pea and bean plants) contain nitrogen-fixing

Lightning

Nitrogen-fixing bacteria in root nodules fix nitrogen into the soil.

Animals eat plants and produce waste.

Decomposers break down dead plants and animals, and animal waste.

Nitrogen-fixing bacteria in the soil fix nitrogen into the soil.

Nitrogen-fixing bacteria help turn nitrogen from plant and animal remains into ammonium.

bacteria. The bacteria contain enzymes that catalyze (speed up) the change of atmospheric nitrogen and hydrogen into a compound called ammonium. Some farmers plant crops that contain these bacteria to avoid using expensive fertilizers.

ANIMALS AND PLANTS

Once the unreactive atmospheric nitrogen has been converted into available compounds in the soil, it is absorbed by plants. The plants are eaten by animals, who are often themselves eaten by another animal. The nitrogen is passed along the food chain and returns to the soil when an animal passes excretions or dies.

DECOMPOSERS

Decomposers include bacteria and fungi. They break down dead animals, plant matter, and the excretions of animals, and produce ammonium.

NITRIFYING BACTERIA

These bacteria use enzymes to turn nitrogen, in the form of ammonium, into nitrates. This process is called **nitrification**. The ammonium comes from the products of the nitrogen-fixing bacteria and also from the remains of dead plants and animals. When plants and animals die, the nitrogen contained in their bodies is recycled back into the soil.

DENITRIFYING BACTERIA

Denitrification occurs when nitrates are turned into atmospheric nitrogen. In soil that does not contain oxygen, denitrifying bacteria carry out this process. The bacteria live in waterlogged soil where oxygen is usually absent. Farmers and gardeners try to avoid this process, as they want to keep their soil nitrogen-rich. Plowing the soil is one way to improve oxygen circulation and prevent denitrification.

Nitrogen in the atmosphere.

Plants take up nitrates from the soil.

Nitrifying bacteria turn ammonium into nitrites and nitrates.

Denitrifying bacteria remove nitrogen from the soil and return it to the atmosphere.

TEST YOURSELF

▶ How do the following practices help improve the condition of soil?

Draining waterlogged soil

Plowing

Using NPK fertilizers

Planting peas or beans

DAMAGING NITROGEN

While nitrogen is essential for most life-forms, including plants, an excess of nitrogen can be very damaging. When fertilizers are used extensively, there can be drastic effects. **Eutrophication** is the gradual increase of nutrients such as nitrogen and phosphorus in the environment. It mainly occurs in aquatic environments, but there is evidence that it also happens in terrestrial environments. Eutrophication forces a change in the **biodiversity** (variety of organisms) in a region.

▲ An algal bloom has taken place in this estuary. The water is polluted with fertilizers, which has led to eutrophication.

EUTROPHICATION

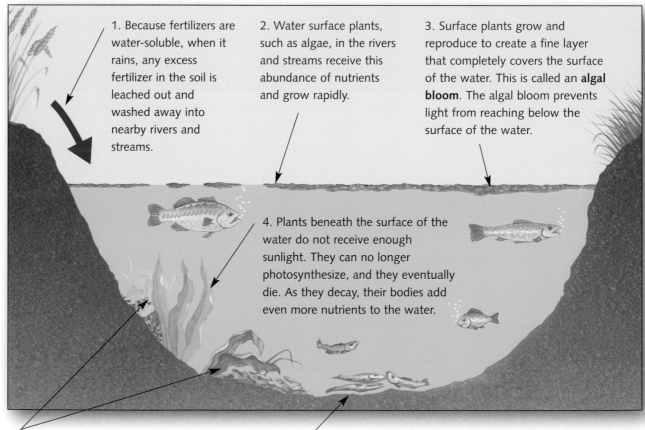

1. Because fertilizers are water-soluble, when it rains, any excess fertilizer in the soil is leached out and washed away into nearby rivers and streams.

2. Water surface plants, such as algae, in the rivers and streams receive this abundance of nutrients and grow rapidly.

3. Surface plants grow and reproduce to create a fine layer that completely covers the surface of the water. This is called an **algal bloom**. The algal bloom prevents light from reaching below the surface of the water.

4. Plants beneath the surface of the water do not receive enough sunlight. They can no longer photosynthesize, and they eventually die. As they decay, their bodies add even more nutrients to the water.

5. Bacteria feed on the dead plants and take in oxygen. This reduces the amount of oxygen in the water. Under normal circumstances, the oxygen used up by the bacteria is replaced by the water plants' photosynthesis products, but this cannot happen when eutrophication occurs.

6. Eventually, the oxygen level is reduced so much that larger organisms cannot meet their own oxygen demands. Small fish are affected first. If they can, they escape to other areas; if they can't, they die. As the numbers of small fish decrease, their predators, such as larger fish higher up in the food chain, are also affected. Their numbers decrease as they cannot get enough food to survive.

A LIVING EXAMPLE

The Mississippi River is the second-longest river in the United States. It begins in Minnesota and flows for 2,320 miles (3,733 km) to Louisiana, where it pours into the Gulf of Mexico. It drains 41 percent of the continental U.S., and every year, about 1.8 million tons (1.6 million t) of nitrogen are added to the river through human activities, such as fertilizer runoff and sewage outlets. The excess nitrogen has caused eutrophication to occur, which has resulted in a "dead zone" at the river's end in the Gulf of Mexico.

Dead zones are extremely low in oxygen and can support almost no life. The dead zone in the Gulf of Mexico was discovered in 1974 and is currently as large as the state of New Jersey. The fish and shrimp have either swum away or died, and bottom-dwellers, such as starfish and anemones, cannot escape and therefore suffocate. Current efforts to reduce the size of the dead zone include encouraging farmers to use less fertilizer. Each of the states surrounding the river is also being given money to update its sewage treatment plants so that nitrogen-containing sewage is not released into the water.

▼ This map of the U.S. shows the extent of the Mississippi's basin and that of its tributaries (smaller rivers to which it is joined).

MISSISSIPPI BASIN

Missouri River

Yellowstone River

Arkansas River

Illinois River

Ohio River

Red River

Mississippi River

Tennessee River

Canadian River

Gulf of Mexico

3

The carbon cycle

Carbon is an essential part of life on Earth. Plants take in carbon in the form of carbon dioxide. During photosynthesis, they use it to create glucose for energy. Animals eat the plants and use the carbon to build their own tissues. Animals return the carbon to the air when they breathe out carbon dioxide and to the ground when they die and decompose. Carbon is constantly recycled—the carbon in your body was once part of the air, an animal, or a plant.

THE CARBON CYCLE

This diagram shows how carbon is recycled between plants, animals, bacteria, the atmosphere, the oceans, and Earth itself.

PLANTS

Green plants remove carbon from the atmosphere, in the form of carbon dioxide, through the process of photosynthesis.

ANIMALS

Animals consume the carbon in plants and use it for energy. They also release carbon dioxide into the atmosphere.

RESPIRATION

This process is carried out by animals and plants, and it releases carbon back into the atmosphere as carbon dioxide. The bacteria that break down the remains of plants and animals also respire aerobically, which means that they release carbon dioxide into the atmosphere.

DECOMPOSITION

When plants and animals die, bacteria break down the tissues, and the plants and animals decompose. Their carbon is returned to the ground and the atmosphere.

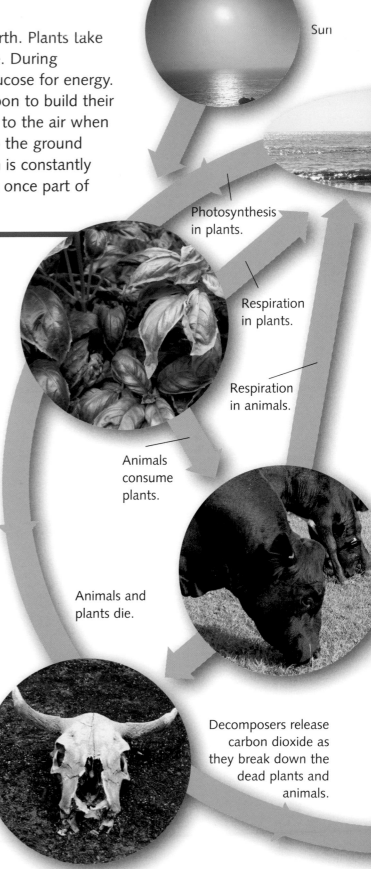

Sun

Photosynthesis in plants.

Respiration in plants.

Respiration in animals.

Animals consume plants.

Animals and plants die.

Decomposers release carbon dioxide as they break down the dead plants and animals.

Carbon dioxide is present in the atmosphere and the oceans.

Geological processes, such as volcanoes and the weathering of rocks, release carbon dioxide.

Combustion of fuels releases carbon dioxide into the atmosphere.

Animals and plants become fossilized. When oceanic organisms die, their bodies fall to the seabed and form a massive store of carbon.

FOSSIL FUELS

Depending on where they die, some animal and plant remains form fossil fuels rather than undergo bacterial decay. The carbon held within the animal or plant is converted into carbon compounds in the fuel. Fossil fuels include coal, oil, and natural gas. Fossil fuels take millions of years to form and require specific conditions to develop, such as the immense pressure and heat created by the overlying rocks and soil.

COMBUSTION

Fossil fuels are a source of energy. Through their combustion (burning), we are provided with energy to power our vehicles, to heat our homes, and to generate electricity. Combustion also releases carbon into the atmosphere in the form of carbon dioxide.

GEOLOGICAL PROCESSES

Not only biological mechanisms are involved in the carbon cycle; geological processes are also important. For example, volcanoes release large amounts of carbon dioxide into the atmosphere, and when rain falls on rock such as chalk, carbon dissolves and runs into Earth's waterways.

OCEANS

Carbon dioxide is a water-soluble gas. Two-thirds of Earth's surface is covered by water, and large amounts of carbon dioxide are dissolved within it. The ocean is called a carbon sink, as it soaks up a lot of carbon dioxide. In addition, the ocean beds are littered with the skeletons of marine creatures, which contain large quantities of carbon.

EXCESS CARBON DIOXIDE

In an ideal world, the processes that remove and return carbon dioxide to the atmosphere would balance each other out. This would allow carbon dioxide levels to stay constant. However, the amount of carbon dioxide in the atmosphere is increasing. The excess carbon dioxide has come from fossil fuel-burning power plants, automobile exhausts, and factories. Each year, man puts more than 24 billion tons (22 billion t) of carbon dioxide and other greenhouse gases, such as water vapor, ozone, and methane, into the atmosphere. Greenhouse gases trap heat in Earth's atmosphere. A natural greenhouse effect is needed to keep our planet warm enough to live on, but our accelerated greenhouse effect is more dangerous.

As Earth is becoming warmer, the ice caps and glaciers are beginning to melt, which is contributing to rising sea levels and changes in ocean currents. In the future, Earth is likely to experience more flooding, and habitats will change, which will threaten the survival of some species. Agriculture and the global economy are also likely to be affected. In addition, when carbon dioxide dissolves in water, it forms an acidic solution that many species cannot tolerate. Marine life could be affected, and many coral reefs may be at risk.

▲ Power stations emit greenhouse gases that contribute to the greenhouse effect.

THE KYOTO PROTOCOL

An international treaty called the Kyoto Protocol was signed in 1997 and came into force in 2005. It states that industrialized countries must reduce their collective greenhouse gas emissions by 5.2 percent compared to 1990 levels. Each country has its own specific target, with those in the European Union (EU) expected to cut emissions by eight percent and Japan by six percent. Some targets are set higher than current emission levels. Russia is one country that can easily meet its target. The protocol permits it to sell its excess "carbon credits" for millions of dollars to countries that don't yet meet their targets. This is called emissions trading. It is hoped that all targets will be reached by 2008 to 2012. Following a historic "meeting of the parties" in Montreal in late 2005, negotiations on a new round of emission reduction targets have begun. This meeting strengthened the Kyoto Protocol. To date, 157 countries have ratified (approved) the agreement, but this does not include the U.S. because President George W. Bush believes that signing would seriously damage the U.S. economy. The U.S.

▲ Environmental activists across the world campaign for the reduction of carbon dioxide emissions.

government described the agreement as "fatally flawed," as it does not require developing countries to reduce emissions. Developing countries are exempt because they were not the main contributors to the greenhouse gas emissions during the industrialization period believed to be causing today's climate change. The U.S. government supports the agreement through developing alternative technologies that do not emit greenhouse gases, although this won't have any effect for a number of years.

THE KYOTO COUNTRIES

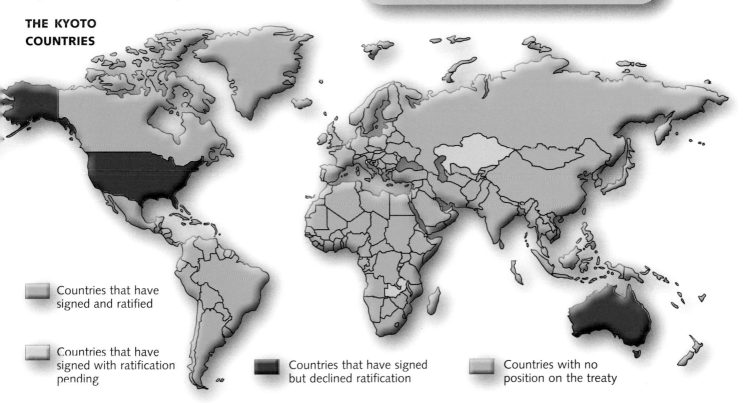

- Countries that have signed and ratified
- Countries that have signed with ratification pending
- Countries that have signed but declined ratification
- Countries with no position on the treaty

HOW ARE EMISSIONS REDUCED?

(1) Development of alternative automobile fuels. Hybrid cars, for example, use fewer fossil fuels because they partly run on battery power.

(2) Congestion charges in large cities, such as London, require people to pay if they want to drive in the city center during certain times of the day. It is hoped that as more people use public transportation, there will be a reduction in carbon dioxide emissions by vehicles.

(3) Emissions trading between developed and developing countries.

(4) Replanting forests reduces the carbon dioxide in the atmosphere because trees take in the gas during photosynthesis. Replanting can also earn a country extra credits under the Kyoto Protocol.

4

Photosynthesis in detail

The word "photo" comes from the Greek word for "light," and "synthesis" means "manufacture." Photosynthesis is a process that uses sunlight to manufacture food. It takes place in the leaves of green plants and is a series of complicated changes in which carbon dioxide and water are converted into oxygen and glucose.

Photosynthesis can be summarized by the following equation:

CHLOROPHYLL AND SUNLIGHT
CARBON DIOXIDE + WATER → GLUCOSE + OXYGEN

Chlorophyll and sunlight are written above the equation because they are both needed for the process, but they do not change form.

CAPTURING SUNLIGHT

Chlorophyll is a pigment found inside compartments called chloroplasts. Chloroplasts are located inside the leaf cells of green plants. Chlorophyll gives green plants their distinctive color. It traps sunlight, which is the driving force for photosynthesis. Leaves contain millions of chloroplasts—the cells in the interior of a leaf contain roughly 325 million chloroplasts for every square inch (6.5 sq cm) of leaf.

The three primary colors of sunlight are red, green, and blue. Chlorophyll absorbs (soaks up) the energy in red and blue light, and it reflects the energy in green light. This is why you see leaves as green.

WHY PLANTS LOOK GREEN

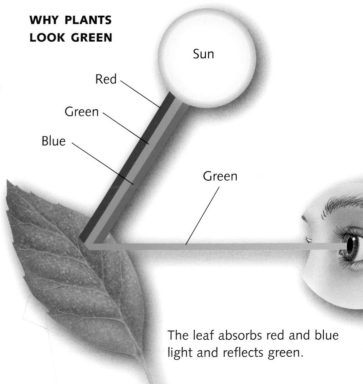

The leaf absorbs red and blue light and reflects green.

PHOTOSYNTHESIS

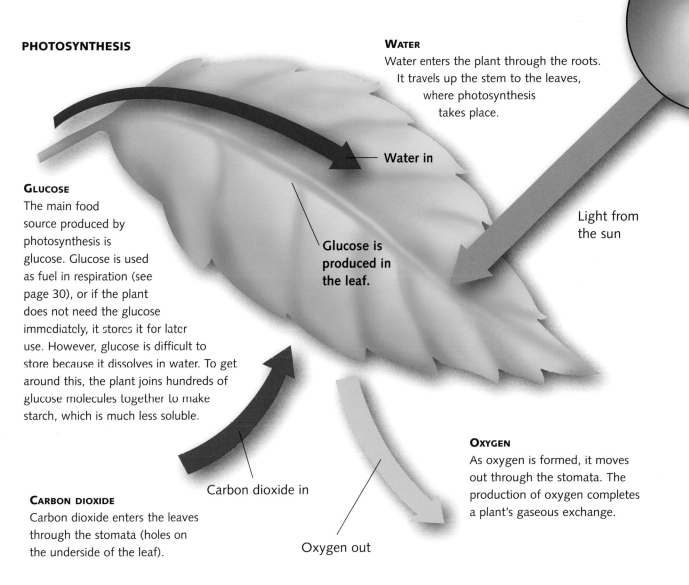

WATER
Water enters the plant through the roots. It travels up the stem to the leaves, where photosynthesis takes place.

Water in

Light from the sun

GLUCOSE
The main food source produced by photosynthesis is glucose. Glucose is used as fuel in respiration (see page 30), or if the plant does not need the glucose immediately, it stores it for later use. However, glucose is difficult to store because it dissolves in water. To get around this, the plant joins hundreds of glucose molecules together to make starch, which is much less soluble.

Glucose is produced in the leaf.

CARBON DIOXIDE
Carbon dioxide enters the leaves through the stomata (holes on the underside of the leaf).

Carbon dioxide in

Oxygen out

OXYGEN
As oxygen is formed, it moves out through the stomata. The production of oxygen completes a plant's gaseous exchange.

INVESTIGATE

▶ How do we know if photosynthesis has taken place? If a plant has successfully carried out photosynthesis, it will contain starch in its leaves. Scientists can test for this by adding iodine solution, which turns blue-black in the presence of starch.

To test a leaf for starch:

(1) Hold a green leaf with a pair of tongs and carefully dip it into boiling water for about one minute. This softens the leaf.

(2) Fill a test tube with ethanol and put this in the hot water. Submerge the leaf in the ethanol to remove the chlorophyll. **Caution: Do not use an exposed flame near the ethanol.**

(3) When all of the chlorophyll has been removed and the leaf looks white, carefully remove it and put it in cold water to soften it again.

(4) Spread the leaf out on a petri dish and flood it with iodine solution. Do not touch the leaf or the iodine with your hands, as this will contaminate the experiment. The areas of the leaf that are blue-black indicate areas where starch has been stored.

PLANT STRUCTURE AND PHOTOSYNTHESIS

Plants are unable to move from place to place to seek out the perfect conditions for photosynthesis. Therefore, their structure must maximize photosynthesis, wherever the plants are located.

LEAF SHAPE

Although leaves come in a huge variety of shapes and sizes, they are almost always flat with a large surface area. The greater the surface area, the more sunlight can be absorbed. Leaves are usually thin, which allows the carbon dioxide to easily reach all of the cells.

▼ Bay leaf

▲ Clover leaf

LEAF POSITION

Leaves are located where sunlight is most readily available. They are positioned around the stem in a spiral pattern, either clockwise or counterclockwise, and where possible, they avoid overlapping one another. Therefore, all of the sunlight that shines onto a plant can be captured.

▲ Leaves are usually arranged around the plant so that they receive as much sunlight as possible.

LEAF CONTENTS

In addition to containing chlorophyll, leaves also contain veins, which transport water to and from the site of photosynthesis. Veins also help to support the leaf and prevent it from wilting. This ensures that it faces the sun and receives the maximum amount of sunlight.

CUTICLE

The top of each leaf is covered in a waterproof layer called a cuticle. This layer prevents the loss of water through evaporation but is colorless so that sunlight can still pass through. The layer does not let gases through; instead, they must enter and leave through the underside of the leaf. Plants that spend their entire life in water do not need a cuticle, whereas those in desert environments are extremely waxy to prevent potentially lethal water loss.

▼ Cacti have a waxy cuticle and spines instead of flat leaves to reduce water loss.

UPPER EPIDERMIS

The upper epidermis is a layer of cells just beneath the cuticle. This layer does not contain any chloroplasts and remains thin so that sunlight can pass straight through it.

PALISADE LAYER

This consists of one or more layers of cylindrical cells standing on their ends like columns. They contain numerous chloroplasts. This is the main site of photosynthesis.

LEAF CROSS-SECTION

LOWER EPIDERMIS

The lower epidermis forms the underside of the leaf. It does not have a cuticle but is covered with stomata. Guard cells control the stomata openings by changing shape. When a stoma is open, water and gases can pass through. When a stoma is closed, water and gases cannot pass through.

Cuticle

Upper epidermis

Palisade cell

Xylem

Phloem

Spongy layer

Guard cell

Stoma

Lower epidermis

SPONGY LAYER

One of the main functions of the cells in this layer is to store the starch produced in photosynthesis. The cells are irregularly shaped and are only loosely packed together. The air spaces between them allow for efficient exchange of carbon dioxide and oxygen. This gaseous exchange occurs by **diffusion**—gases move from areas of high concentration to areas of low concentration.

TEST YOURSELF

▶ Make a summary table to show how plants and leaves are adapted to photosynthesis. Include information on the structure of plants, and describe the role of each layer of the leaf.

EVIDENCE FOR PHOTOSYNTHESIS

The requirements for and products of photosynthesis have been demonstrated by scientists through simple experiments, which are outlined below.

(1) HOW DO WE KNOW CHLOROPHYLL IS VITAL FOR PHOTOSYNTHESIS?

Some plants have variegated leaves, which means that some areas contain chlorophyll and look green, and other areas do not contain chlorophyll and look white. Such plants are ideal for determining whether chlorophyll is necessary for photosynthesis. If chlorophyll is vital, starch will be produced in the green parts and not in the white parts.

▼ Variegated leaves are used for some experiments because they have areas that contain no chlorophyll.

PROCEDURE

(1) De-starch a plant with variegated leaves by putting it in complete darkness for 48 hours. The plant will use up its stored starch and will not make any new starch.

(2) Expose the plant to sunshine for a few hours.

(3) Test a few leaves for the presence of starch (see page 21).

Note: A de-starched plant is one that has used up all of the starch stored in the leaves through respiration.

RESULTS

Some parts of the leaf will look blue-black; others will look red-brown.

CONCLUSION

Any starch in the plant has been produced by photosynthesis during the experiment. Starch is produced only in the areas where chlorophyll was originally found. Therefore, we know that chlorophyll is vital for photosynthesis.

(2) HOW DO WE KNOW THAT CARBON DIOXIDE IS REQUIRED FOR PHOTOSYNTHESIS?

This experiment also begins with a de-starched plant.

PROCEDURE

(1) Place some soda lime in a plastic bag. Soda lime extracts carbon dioxide from the atmosphere.

(2) Put the de-starched plant inside the plastic bag and secure the top with a rubber band. This keeps the atmosphere around the plant carbon dioxide-free.

(3) Leave the plant in sunlight for a few hours.

(4) Remove a few leaves and test for starch (see page 21).

RESULTS

The leaves look red-brown in color.

CONCLUSIONS

The plant in this experiment was deprived of carbon dioxide. Therefore, it was not able to photosynthesize and produce starch. Photosynthesis cannot proceed without carbon dioxide.

(3) HOW DO WE KNOW THAT OXYGEN IS PRODUCED DURING PHOTOSYNTHESIS?

This experiment uses a water-dwelling plant.

▲ Water-dwelling plants extract carbon dioxide from the water and release oxygen back into the water.

PROCEDURE

(1) Collect a sample of pondweed and put it in a beaker of water.

(2) Put a funnel upside down over the pondweed. Place a test tube over the top of the funnel.

(3) Leave the apparatus in sunlight for a few hours.

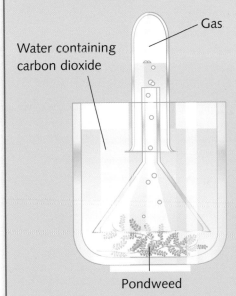

Gas

Water containing carbon dioxide

Pondweed

(4) Carefully remove the test tube, but do not turn it up the right way, as this will let the gas escape.

(5) Carefully light a wooden splint, then blow out the flame. While the splint is still glowing, put it in the test tube and observe what happens.

RESULTS

The glowing splint relights.

CONCLUSIONS

For a glowing splint to relight, there must be a relatively high concentration of oxygen. Therefore, the pondweed took in carbon dioxide from the water, photosynthesized, and released oxygen, which collected in the boiling tube. Oxygen is produced during photosynthesis.

(4) How do we know that sunlight is needed for photosynthesis?

This experiment demonstrates that within one leaf, some parts photosynthesize, while other parts do not, depending on the availability of sunlight.

Procedure

(1) Cut out a stencil in aluminum foil or black paper.

(2) Put the stencil over one leaf of a de-starched plant. Use paper clips to hold it in place.

(3) Leave the plant in sunlight for at least one day.

(4) Remove the test leaf and the stencil, and test for starch (see page 21).

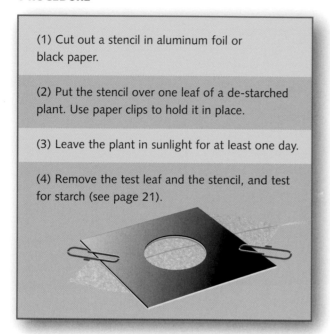

Results

The leaf has a red-brown area the same shape as the paper that covered it. The part of the leaf that was exposed to sunlight is blue-black.

Conclusion

The area under the stencil has not photosynthesized. Starch is produced only in the areas of the leaf exposed to sunlight. Therefore, sunlight is vital for photosynthesis.

Test yourself

▶ Why do most of these experiments use de-starched plants?
▶ How would the results be affected if you did not use de-starched plants?

MANIPULATING PHOTOSYNTHESIS

Professional growers, such as farmers and gardeners, try to create conditions that will maximize their plants' photosynthesis. This enables them to boost their profits and maintain an income for as much of the year as possible. For example, strawberries are a summer fruit, but by manipulating photosynthesis, growers can produce strawberries in the winter. Some commercial growth is carried out in a greenhouse. Greenhouses provide a controlled environment and protection from adverse conditions.

How do greenhouses work?

Greenhouses are enclosed and offer protection from herbivores, such as rabbits and slugs. Conditions inside the greenhouse are easily controlled and can be completely different from conditions outside the greenhouse. If a greenhouse is heated, the temperature is kept warm inside as long as doors and windows remain closed. Greenhouses also use a lot of natural sunlight to keep them warm. Light passes through the glass, but it cannot leave in the same way. The glass changes the sunlight so that it does not have enough energy to pass back out through the glass. Therefore, the heat from the sun's rays becomes trapped inside the greenhouse.

Making conditions right

Light – Growers use the sun's natural light for the plants inside to photosynthesize. During the night, plants cannot naturally photosynthesize. Growers may use an artificial light to maintain photosynthesis 24 hours a day.

Temperature – Up to a specific temperature, plants photosynthesize faster the warmer it is. However, if temperatures reach 104 °F to 122 °F (40-50 °C), the rate of photosynthesis slows down.

▶ Greenhouses, such as this enormous one at the Eden Project in the UK, allow growers to create the conditions necessary to cultivate almost any type of plant.

This is because a plant's enzymes **denature** at high temperatures. The structure of the enzyme changes, and it can no longer function. Heat cannot easily escape through glass, so many greenhouses have windows that can be opened and closed; sometimes this is controlled thermostatically. This means that they automatically open when the temperature gets too high and close when it is too cool. When temperatures are very low, electric heaters are used. Overall, the plants are subjected to the optimum temperatures required for photosynthesis.

Carbon dioxide – The more carbon dioxide is present, the greater the rate of photosynthesis. Commercial growers may pump carbon dioxide directly into the greenhouse. Or, they may use kerosene heaters, which have two main benefits. They increase the greenhouse temperature and release carbon dioxide as a by-product of kerosene combustion.

Water – Many greenhouses have automatic watering systems similar to garden sprinklers. The system switches water on for set periods each day to prevent the plants from drying out.

TEST YOURSELF

▶ Give three reasons why lettuces are grown in tunnels made from clear polyethylene plastic?

DID YOU KNOW?

▶ An exotic globe spear lily blossomed for the first time after an incredible 23 years inside a greenhouse in Belfast, Ireland. This type of lily is always slow-growing and is usually found in the wild in Australia. The plant in Belfast is much taller than average because of the optimum growing conditions employed in the greenhouse.

Plants and water

Water is important for plants for two reasons. First, it provides plants with support and prevents wilting. Second, although most of a plant's food requirements are satisfied through photosynthesis, some nutrients must be gained from soil moisture. Water-soluble nutrients taken in by the roots are vital to a plant's healthy growth.

ENTERING THE PLANT

A plant's roots secure the plant in the soil and seek out water. Water and its dissolved mineral nutrients enter through the roots. Roots can be very powerful, and some very old trees are responsible for lifting buildings and roads as their roots grow in their search for water. Roots are covered with fine hair-like structures called root hairs. The root hairs increase the surface area

ROOT HAIR CELL
Actual root hair cell length is between 0.003 and 0.06 inches (0.08-1.5 mm).

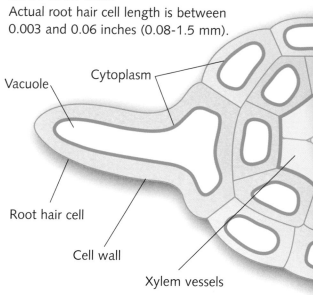

Vacuole

Cytoplasm

Root hair cell

Cell wall

Xylem vessels

across which water can pass into the plant.

Water enters the root by a specialized type of diffusion called osmosis. Osmosis usually involves the movement of water across a semipermeable membrane. Semipermeable membranes allow only specific substances to pass. In a root, water and its dissolved mineral nutrients move from where water is plentiful to where water is less plentiful. They move into the root hair cell and are drawn across the root cells until they reach the xylem vessel. The water is drawn up the xylem to the rest of the plant.

◄ These powerful roots are growing over a stone building in an attempt to reach soil and moisture.

TRANSPIRATION

Around 98 percent of all water that enters a plant through its roots is lost into the atmosphere by evaporation from the leaves. The loss of water at the leaves provides a force that helps to pull water up through the xylem. The greater the loss of water from the leaves, the more water is drawn up through the xylem and ultimately into the roots. This movement of water through the plant is called **transpiration**. A piece of equipment called a potometer is used to measure the rate of transpiration. A cutting is placed into the potometer and an air bubble is introduced into the equipment. As the cutting transpires, it pulls water into its roots, and the bubble moves through the potometer. Once the clock starts, the movement of the bubble is measured for a specific period of time. The farther the bubble moves, the greater the rate of transpiration.

POTOMETER EXPERIMENT

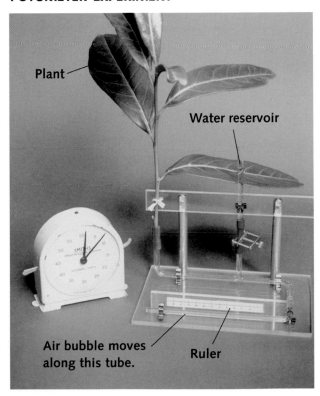

Plant

Water reservoir

Air bubble moves along this tube.

Ruler

▲ The reservoir is used to refill the equipment at the end of the experiment.

▲ Plants in hot and windy climates have rapid transpiration rates.

FACTORS THAT AFFECT TRANSPIRATION

Atmospheric conditions influence the rate of transpiration, and the effects of these conditions can be measured using a potometer.

1) Wind — Wind increases the transpiration rate. When water reaches the surface of the leaf, it evaporates, and the wind quickly carries it away. Water is drawn up to take its place, so the rate of transpiration increases.

2) Light intensity and temperature — A very sunny day increases evaporation from the leaf, as the sunlight causes the stomata to open to allow photosynthesis. This means that more water is lost, and the transpiration rate increases. Higher temperatures also increase the amount of water the surrounding air can hold. As a result, more water evaporates from the leaf, and the transpiration rate increases.

3) Humidity — If the air surrounding the leaf is humid and already holds a lot of water, less can evaporate from the leaf by diffusion. The transpiration rate therefore decreases.

Plant respiration

In nature, green plants are not exposed to sunlight 24 hours a day. During the night, they cannot photosynthesize, and instead rely on another process—respiration. Respiration uses oxygen to release the energy in glucose. Carbon dioxide and water are produced during respiration. This is summarized by the following equation:

Oxygen + Glucose → Energy + Carbon Dioxide + Water

Respiration is the opposite of photosynthesis, but they can both occur at the same time. Photosynthesis provides food, and respiration releases the food's energy for the processes of life, such as growth and reproduction.

PHOTOSYNTHESIS VERSUS RESPIRATION

Full daylight – The rate of photosynthesis is greater than the rate of respiration. More food is produced than is consumed.

Dim light – The rates of photosynthesis and respiration are approximately equal. Food is produced at about the same rate as it is consumed. The point at which they are exactly equal is called the **compensation point**.

Darkness – No photosynthesis occurs. Respiration continues, and food that has been produced and stored in the plant is used up. A plant that is left in total darkness for about 48 hours will use up all of its stored food.

RESPIRATION GASES

Photosynthesis requires carbon dioxide and releases oxygen. Respiration requires oxygen and releases carbon dioxide. The exchange of gases takes place via the stomata on the underside of the leaves. The gases move easily through the air spaces of the spongy layer.

RESPIRATION GASES

Bright light   Dim light   Darkness

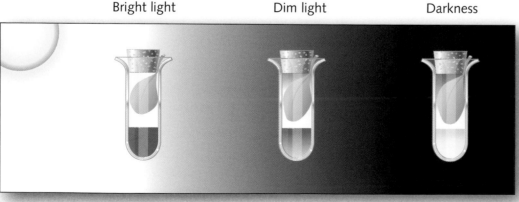

Bright light – Photosynthesis dominates, and carbon dioxide is taken in. The indicator turns purple.

Dim light – At the compensation point, there is no overall change in the carbon dioxide levels. The indicator remains red.

Darkness – Respiration exceeds photosynthesis, and carbon dioxide is produced. The indicator turns yellow.

Experiments can show the gas exchange. Carbon dioxide is an acidic gas. Its presence turns a hydrogen carbonate chemical indicator yellow. A lack of carbon dioxide turns the indicator purple. Hydrogen carbonate is usually red.

Plant growth

Plants are sensitive to their environments. However, this sensitivity is not always obvious because it occurs more slowly than in animals. Plants are sensitive to light, water, and gravity. Their responses are controlled by plant hormones.

SENSITIVITY—TROPISMS

Houseplants in sunny windows grow toward the light. Growth that is affected by light is called **phototropism**. When plants grow toward light, this is described as positive phototropism. Growth away from light is described as negative phototropism. The growth is caused by plant hormones called **auxins**, which are found in the tips of roots and shoots. We know this because when the tip of a shoot or root is removed, the remainder of the root or shoot stops growing. When the tip is replaced, it begins to grow again.

▲ These sunflowers are showing positive phototropism.

SHOWING THE ACTION OF
LIGHT-SENSITIVE AUXINS

Auxins are light-sensitive. When a plant receives light from all angles, the auxins produced in the tip evenly distribute themselves down both sides of the plant so that all cells are affected equally. The cells are the same size and dimension, and growth is even.

When the plant receives light from one side, the auxins from the tip are unequally distributed. Most diffuse down the darker side of the tip. The cells that receive more auxins absorb more water and increase in size. As the cells grow larger, they begin to divide. The side with auxins becomes bigger and pushes the tip toward the light.

Seedlings in complete darkness contain auxins and are capable of growth. However, they can not photosynthesize, but rely on food already stored in their seeds or leaves. Growth is slow and straight, as there is no light to redistribute the auxins. If the seedlings remain in the dark, they will die when all of the food is used up.

FACING THE SUN

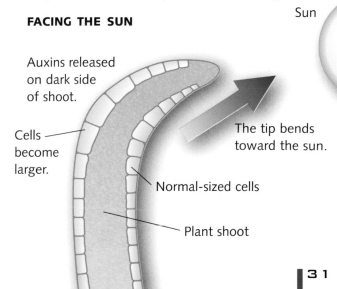

Sun

Auxins released on dark side of shoot.

Cells become larger.

The tip bends toward the sun.

Normal-sized cells

Plant shoot

OTHER PLANT HORMONES

Auxins are not the only plant hormones. Although most hormones promote growth, other hormones influence the ripening of fruit, release a seed's food store to allow it to grow into a new plant, or even inhibit growth during times of stress. Scientists have manufactured synthetic plant hormones for a variety of uses by commercial growers.

Use	Details
Synchronized fruiting	One ripe fruit in a bowl usually causes others to ripen. A synthetic hormone causes the same effect in fruit trees. It makes machine fruit-picking more efficient because all of the fruit ripens at once.
Weed killers	High concentrations of hormones upset growth. Weeds are sensitive to this, and the application of hormones can kill them. This can be selective, as each weed species is sensitive to a different quantity of hormones.
Cuttings	Plant cuttings can be treated with hormones to make them develop into new plants. This is an important way of producing new plants. The cut stem is covered in growth hormone and planted. The hormone encourages roots to grow.

INVESTIGATE

▶ Sprinkle some watercress seeds on damp tissue or cotton. When seedlings appear, place them in a sunny window. Observe after a few days. What happens to the seedlings and why?

Next, turn the seedlings around by 180° and observe after a few days. What happens and why? Grow a new batch of watercress seedlings. When the shoots appear, place them in total darkness. Observe them after a few days. What happens to the shoots?

TIME TRAVEL: DISCOVERIES OF THE PAST

CHARLES DARWIN AND PLANT HORMONES

Charles Darwin (right), the famous scientist who helped unlock some of the secrets of **evolution**, was also one of the first scientists to observe the effects of plant auxins. In 1880, he wrote a book entitled *The Power of Movement in Plants*. In it, he described the effect that light had on canary grass seedlings when light was shone from one direction—the canary grass bent toward the light source. He experimented by covering the tips of the grass with foil and discovered that no bending occurred. But his breakthrough experiment involved covering the area just beneath the tip and leaving the tip uncovered. This resulted in bending, and he concluded that the tip itself detected light and sent a signal to the area just beneath it, which resulted in the seedlings bending toward the light.

Plant reproduction

To ensure the continuation of a plant species, plants must reproduce. Flowers contain the plant's sex organs. Most plants reproduce sexually. This means that two **gametes** (sex cells), one male and one female, fuse and develop to form a new individual.

FLOWER STRUCTURE

Most flowers contain both the male and female sex organs and gametes.

Structure	Role
Petals	Attract insects to the flower
Sepals	Protect flower buds
Nectary	Produces sugary nectar for insects
Stamen	Male sex organs that produce pollen—made up of the anther and filament
Anther	Makes the male gametes (pollen)
Filament	Holds the anther in position
Carpel	Female sex organs that produce female gametes (eggs)—made up of the stigma, style, and ovary
Stigma	Top of the carpel, and the place where the pollen lands in pollination
Ovary	Contain the female gametes

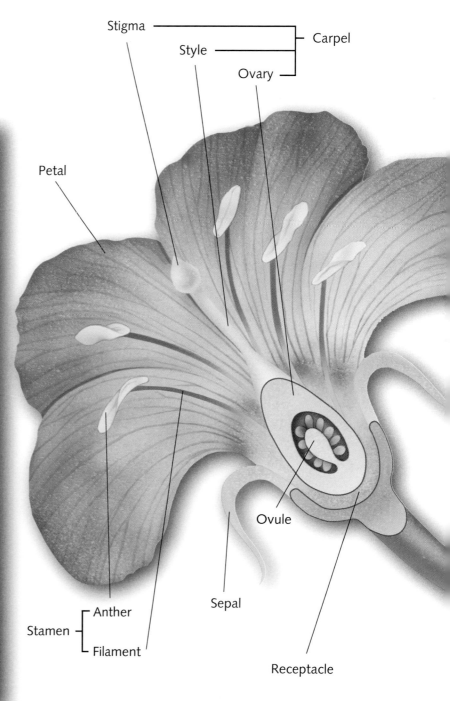

LIFE CYCLE OF A FLOWERING PLANT

Flowering plants go through each of the following stages in their life cycle:

Pollination – Transfer of pollen to stigma.

Fertilization – Fusion of male and female gametes.

Seed dispersal – The relocation of seeds.

Germination – Growth of a seed into a plant.

POLLINATION

Pollination is the transfer of pollen from the male anther to the sticky top of the carpel, called the stigma. Pollen grains contain the plant's male gametes and are produced in the anthers. The anthers are positioned at the top of the filaments. Together, an anther and a filament are called a stamen. When the pollen grains are ripe, the anther splits and releases its pollen. The female gametes are located in the ovules, which are found in the ovary at the base of the carpel.

METHODS OF POLLINATION

Pollen can be transferred by the wind or by insects.

INSECT POLLINATION

Plants that rely on insects to carry their pollen usually have the following features:

(1) Colorful petals and sweet-smelling nectar. These attract insects to the flowers. Insects enter the flowers in search of nectar, and as they do so, pollen rubs onto their bodies. As they travel from flower to flower, pollen rubs off their bodies and onto the flowers.

(2) Sticky and rough pollen. This helps the pollen stick to the insects.

(3) Some flowers have lines that radiate from the center of the flower, and others have clearly marked "landing platforms." Both of these strategies are designed to attract the insects to the center of the flower.

▶ The bee enters the flower, and pollen rubs onto his legs and back.

WIND POLLINATION

Plants that rely on the wind to transfer their pollen usually have the following features:

(1) The anthers hang outside the flower so that even a gentle breeze will dislodge the pollen.

(2) The style and stigma of the carpel also hang outside the flower. In this way, pollen on the wind may come into contact with them.

(3) The pollen of wind-pollinated plants is smooth and lightweight and can be easily carried by the wind.

(4) These plants do not usually have brightly colored petals or nectar, and some have no petals at all because they do not need to attract insects.

▼ Grasses are wind-pollinated plants. Their seeds are lightweight, and they do not have colorful flowers.

The movement of pollen from one plant to another of the same species is called **cross-pollination**. Other plants are **self-pollinating**, and the pollen from one flower can fertilize the ovum (egg cell) of another flower on the same plant. A second plant is not required. Some plants, such as holly bushes, are entirely male or entirely female. To ensure that pollination will take place, a male and female bush must be in relatively close proximity to each other.

FERTILIZATION

Once pollination has taken place, **fertilization** can begin. Fertilization is the fusion of the male and female gametes, which results in the formation of seeds and fruits.

(1) A pollen grain lands on the stigma. The stigma allows only pollen grains from the same species to continue with the fertilization process.

(2) A pollen tube grows down through the style to the ovary. The male genetic material (the nucleus of the gamete) passes down this channel.

(3) The ovule inside the ovary contains the ovum. The rest of the ovule is a food store.

(4) The male gamete fertilizes (fuses with) the female ovum.

(5) Once fertilization has occurred, a chemical message is sent to the flower so that the next stage of reproduction can occur.

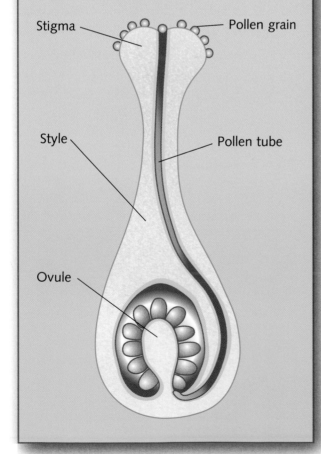

Stigma

Pollen grain

Style

Pollen tube

Ovule

Some flowers, such as those on a plum tree, contain one ovule. However, some flowers, such as poppies, contain thousands of ovules. Each ovule needs its own pollen tube and male gamete for fertilization to occur. Once fertilization is complete, the flower has done its job, and the petals, stamen, stigma, and style wither and fall off.

SEED FORMATION

The fertilized ovum divides to produce a ball of many cells, which forms the embryo of the new plant. The surrounding ovule forms the seed. An ovary can contain many small seeds or one large seed. Large seeds have a plentiful food store for use by the new plant as it develops. Small, abundant seeds have only a little food, but because the seeds are small and easily dispersed, there is a good chance that some of them will develop into a new plant.

Seeds are surrounded by a hard coat that prevents the embryo inside from injury and from drying out. This coat is called the testa. There is a small hole, called a micropyle, in the end of the testa. This allows oxygen and water to enter the seed, which triggers the seed to develop into a new plant. The embryo consists of a plumule, which will become the shoot, and the radicle, which will become the root. Some seeds can lie dormant for many years, which means that they do not change or grow.

FRUIT AND NUT FORMATION

A fruit is an ovary filled with fertile seeds. In some plant species, the ovary forms a fleshy and succulent fruit. In others, it develops into a hard, dry fruit called a nut. Fruits have many uses. They can form a protective coating around the seed, provide the seed with a food supply, and help seed dispersal (see pages 38–40).

Fruits that form from the ovary wall, such as cherries and plums, are called true fruits. True fruits can be either succulent or dry. Succulent fruits are brightly colored and fleshy, such as oranges and peaches. Dry fruits, such as beans and acorns, may split open when they are ripe. Fruits that form from the part below the ovary—the receptacle—are called false fruits. These fruits are fleshy and include pears, apples, and strawberries. Some fruits are incorrectly called vegetables. For example, tomatoes, cucumbers, and peppers are all fruits, not vegetables.

CORN SEED CROSS-SECTION

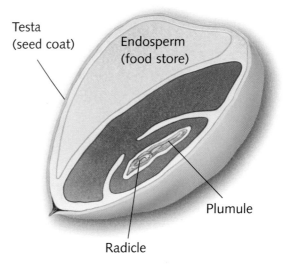

Testa (seed coat)

Endosperm (food store)

Plumule

Radicle

▲ A large number of seeds can be clearly seen in these slices of kiwi fruit.

DID YOU KNOW?

▶ The largest seed in the world is that of the double coconut, the coco-de-mer, which can take up to 10 years to develop. The seed, which weighs up to 44 pounds (20 kg), is native to the Seychelles Islands.

▶ Scientists in Israel have brought a piece of history back to life by successfully growing a date palm plant from a 2,000-year-old seed. The seed was found during archaeological excavations at King Herod's palace on Mount Masada, near the Dead Sea in

Israel. It is believed to be the oldest seed ever found. Previously, the date palm plant was thought to have become extinct in the Middle Ages. The scientists soaked the seed in warm water to soften it. Then they added plant growth hormone, another hormone to encourage root growth, and fertilizer. Unexpectedly, five weeks later, the seed sprouted. The scientists hope that the tree is female and will one day produce dates.

◀ Coco-de-mer seeds take over a year to germinate.

SEED DISPERSAL

Plants require the correct environmental conditions to grow well. Ideally, they do not want to compete with other plants for sunlight, water, and nutrients. Therefore, plants disperse (spread) their seeds over a wide area. Most plants also produce many seeds to ensure that at least some fall onto fertile soil and develop into healthy new plants. There are several methods of dispersal— wind, animal, water, and self-dispersal.

WIND DISPERSAL

Some seeds are carried far from the parent plant by the wind. The seeds need to be lightweight and stay in the air for as long as possible. A dandelion flower forms many tiny, feathery seeds. The fine hairs form a kind of parachute on the end of each stem. The seeds are only loosely attached to the plant so that a breeze can disperse them a surprisingly long distance. Most seeds are carried more than 330 feet (100 m), and some are carried by the wind for more than 0.6 miles (1 km).

▲ This is a close-up of a poppy head. Each poppy flower produces numerous tiny seeds.

Sycamore, elm, and ash tree seeds have "wings," and as the seeds fall, the wings spin. This causes the seeds to fall slowly, which increases the chance that a gust of wind will move them some distance from the parent tree. Poppy flowers are attached to very long stems, which sway in the wind. Poppy seeds are tiny and numerous, and as the stem sways, the poppy head shakes the seeds over a relatively large area.

◀ Dandelion seeds are shaped like parachutes. Humans also play a part in their dispersal when they blow on them.

ANIMAL DISPERSAL

Animal dispersal works in four different ways, depending on the plant. Animals sometimes eat entire fruits, including the seeds. The fruit passes through the animal's digestive system, but the seeds are not digested because the seed coats are too tough. The seeds are excreted in the feces at a new location, usually far from the parent plant, where they can grow into a new plant.

When a fruit contains a large seed, the animal eats only the fleshy part and leaves the seed behind, ready to grow into a new plant.

Some animals bury seeds. For example, squirrels collect acorns, then bury them as a food store for the winter. If the squirrel does not return to the food store, the acorns may grow into new trees.

Some seeds cling to an animal's fur. Burdock seeds are covered with hooks that stick to an animal's fur. As the animal travels from place to place, it carries the seeds with it. When the animal lies down, rolls, or cleans itself, the seeds are dislodged and may grow into a new plant.

▲ This hairy saki monkey disperses palm fruit seeds in the forests of the western Amazon rain forest in South America.

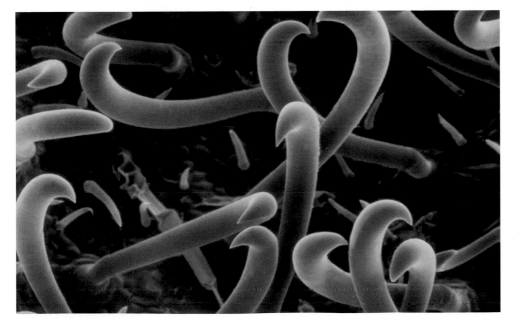

◀ This photograph of a burdock seed has been magnified 55 times. You can clearly see its hooks. The hooks latch on to an animal's fur to help the seed cling on long enough to be transported far from the parent plant.

SELF-DISPERSAL

Some plants, such as lupins and geraniums, disperse their own seeds. As the fruit dries up following fertilization, it explosively splits open, and the seeds are propelled a great distance away.

▼ These geranium seeds are being flung away from the plant. If they land a far enough distance away, the offspring will not compete with the parent plant for light, nutrients, and water.

WATER DISPERSAL

Some plants use water to disperse their seeds. Coconut seeds have a light ovary wall and contain air. This allows them to float in water. If a coconut falls from a tree into a river or the ocean, it can be carried thousands of miles before it washes up and grows into a new tree.

INVESTIGATE

▶ Scientists have discovered why chilies are so hot. Chilies produce a substance called capsaicin, which tastes hot and peppery to mammals. So, mammals avoid eating chilies. Birds, however, cannot taste the capsaicin. Therefore, birds eat the chilies. Birds often travel farther afield than mammals, and this means that they disperse the chili seeds in their feces over a wide area. Scientists suggest that chilies evolved to taste hot so that they would be more widely dispersed. In addition, mammals can digest the seeds and birds cannot—another reason why chili plants want to discourage mammals from eating them!

GERMINATION

Germination occurs when a seed grows into a new plant. Seeds contain a food supply to provide energy for their initial development. Germination does not rely on sunlight. For a seed to germinate, it must have the following:

Water
Oxygen
Suitable temperature for the seed enzymes to work. Many seeds do not grow until the spring when temperatures increase.

FROM DORMANCY TO GERMINATION

A seed can remain dormant for many years and will not germinate until conditions are right. When temperatures are warm enough, the seed's micropyle allows water and oxygen to enter. This converts the insoluble food store into water-soluble food, which can be used by the growing seedling. This process is controlled by temperature-dependent enzymes. The influx of water also makes the seed tissues swell by up to 80 percent so that the seed coat eventually splits open. As the seed coat splits, more water and oxygen can enter the seed, and respiration begins to provide more energy for growth.

ORDER OF GROWTH

The radicle is the first part of the new seedling to grow. It pushes down into the soil. It does not matter which way a seed is planted; the radicle always grows downward. This is an example of another type of tropism, called **geotropism**, which means sensitivity to gravity. Geotropism is controlled by auxins. Roots are more sensitive to auxins than shoots, and only very small amounts are needed to promote growth. In roots, the auxins collect on the lower side and cause downward growth. The opposite is true for shoots.

The plumule appears next. Its tip is slightly bent for protection. The shoot demonstrates negative geotropism as it grows against gravity. The new shoot and root continue to grow, and as the shoot breaks through the soil surface, it straightens out, and its leaves unfold. The plant is now able to photosynthezise and make its own food. At about the same time, the roots begin to branch in search of water. Seedlings are small and fragile, and are at risk of being trampled on, eaten, or damaged by a harsh environment, such as strong winds. Those that survive usually go on to produce flowers and seeds of their own and ensure the continuation of the species.

GROWTH OF A SEEDLING

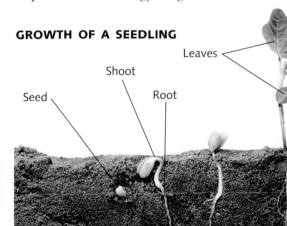

Seed
Shoot
Root
Leaves
Roots

ASEXUAL REPRODUCTION

Not all plants reproduce sexually. Some plants reproduce asexually. **Asexual reproduction** only requires one parent, and the new individual is identical to the parent. In plants, asexual reproduction is called vegetative reproduction and allows one part of the plant, other than a seed, to develop into a new plant. For example, potato, onion, and strawberry plants reproduce asexually.

Potatoes are an extension of a potato plant's root system and are called tubers. If you have ever left a potato in a dark cupboard for a few weeks, you know that it spontaneously grows roots and a shoot even without being planted in soil. Strawberries send out runners that grow along the surface of the soil. A runner can put down roots and grow into a new strawberry plant. Plants that carry out vegetative reproduction can reproduce rapidly and quickly colonize an area of soil.

▼ Onions do not need two parent plants to reproduce. They carry out asexual reproduction.

Uses for plants

Plants supply us with not only oxygen to breathe and food to eat; they are also the source of a surprising array of other everyday items. Rubber, cotton, paper, and many medicines come directly from plants. Aspirin originally came from the bark of willow trees, and cranberries are known for their beneficial effect on some bladder infections. In some parts of the world, sugarcane plants have successfully been made into fuel for cars. Plants also provide invaluable habitats for organisms such as insects, birds, and small mammals.

PLANTS AS MATERIALS

Plants have been used to build shelter for centuries. Homes are still made almost entirely from wood in many areas of the world, such as the U.S. In other places, such as the UK, many homes have a wooden frame around which bricks are secured.

Rubber is an important by-product of plants. More than half of all rubber is synthetic, but several million tons of natural rubber are still collected each year, mainly in Asia. Natural rubber comes from the Para rubber tree, *Hevea brasiliensis*. When the bark of this tree is cut, sap oozes from the wound. In addition, even more sap is produced as a response to damage to the bark. The milky liquid sap, known as latex, is collected and forms the basis of rubber. In places where coconuts are abundant, such as parts of southern India, coconut shells are used to collect the latex. A sharp stick acts as a channel down which the latex drips from the cut in the bark. The latex is mixed with formic acid, which makes it coagulate (turn into a semisolid). It is wrung out and sent to factories, where it is processed to make it smooth, tough, and less resistant to attack by other chemicals.

▲ Latex is collected from the Para rubber tree by cutting the tree and allowing the latex to drip down into a coconut shell.

Another important plant product is paper. The main ingredient of paper is wood pulp, which is the mashed-up wood from softwood trees, such as spruces (pine trees). Other vegetable fibers, such as flax and jute, are also used to make paper. All of the plant fibers are mashed into pulp, washed, and then placed onto a wire mesh. Any remaining water is drained off, and the sheet of paper is dried and cut into rectangular pieces.

Vegetable fibers are also used to make fabrics. Flax, also known as linseed, is one of the oldest fiber crops in the world and has been used to produce linen for around 5,000 years. Jute is one of the cheapest natural plant fibers. It is long and shiny and is also called burlap. Cotton is a naturally soft plant fiber that grows around the seed heads of cotton plants. Cotton production is thought to date back around 14,000 years to Egyptian times. Today, the cotton industry is massive—cotton is produced in Europe, the U.S., Africa, Asia, and Australia. In the U.S., the annual production of cotton is around 23 million tons (21 million t) and is worth around $20 billion.

◄ This jute fiber has been woven into a mat.

PLANTS AS MEDICINES

Many medicines are either extracted directly from plants or derived from plant compounds. Today, around 121 prescription drugs sold worldwide come directly or indirectly from plants. The U.S. National Cancer Institute has identified 3,000 plants that are active against cancer cells, and 70 percent of these plants are found in rain forests. For example, vincristine is one of the world's most powerful anticancer drugs. It is extracted from the rain forest plant periwinkle, which is found in Madagascar. It is effective against acute childhood leukemia and Hodgkin's disease. In total, 25 percent of Western pharmaceuticals are derived from rain forest ingredients, and despite the growing realization that plants can be effective medicines, scientists have to date tested less than one percent of tropical trees and plants.

The rain forests are being cut down for timber and paper, and to make way for agriculture. Rain forests used to cover 14 percent of Earth's surface, but today they cover just six percent, and it is thought that natural rain forests could disappear by the middle of this century. It is vitally important to preserve the rain forests of the world. They release massive quantities of oxygen, take in huge quantities of carbon dioxide, and are potentially home to thousands more life-saving medicines.

PLANTS AS HABITATS

Trees and shrubs house many organisms. They provide protection from predation and shelter from harsh climates. Without plant homes, many organisms would face extinction. Across the

▼ Rain forest plants are sources of medicines and oxygen, and they provide habitats for birds, mammals, and insects.

world, ancient forests are disappearing rapidly. It is not only rain forests that are under threat from being cleared for cattle and firewood. Twenty percent of the world's ancient forests have been cleared since 1950, and those in Indonesia and central Africa could be entirely gone in a few decades. Scientists estimate that 24 percent of mammals, 12 percent of birds, and 14 percent of plants face extinction. Most of these extinction threats are because of habitat destruction of primarily ancient forests.

Occasionally, and on a smaller scale, overgrown habitats can be threatening to a species. A woods in Wales, for example, became so overgrown that a colony of dormice struggled to find sufficient food and water. The woods has since been given an overhaul thanks to volunteers, and the dormouse population is now rising.

OTHER USES FOR PLANTS

Automobiles usually run on gasoline or diesel fuel, which are derived from crude oil. Earth's reserves of crude oil are dwindling, and prices are rising, which has forced people to look for alternative fuels for their vehicles. In Brazil, about 40 percent of all the fuel used for vehicles comes from pure ethanol (alcohol), which is derived from sugarcane. Sugarcane grows well in Brazil—there are already 13.5 million acres (5.5 million ha) planted, and 200 million acres (81 million ha) lie ready to be cultivated. Ethanol fuel is less than half the price of gas and does not contribute as much pollution to the environment. Because of this success, small planes and some power stations in Brazil also use ethanol from sugarcane as their fuel.

▼ The ancient forests (dark green) on these maps are those that have large and intact ecosystems. Other forests exist throughout the world, but in an altered form. Some may not have the full range of organisms that they once did, or they may be fully or partially managed by humans.

FORESTS 8,000 YEARS AGO

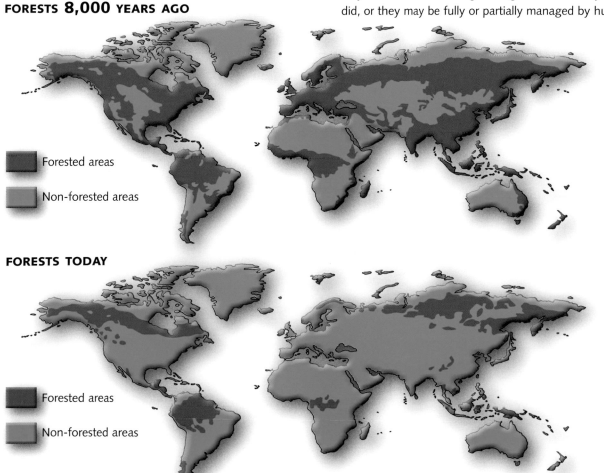

Forested areas

Non-forested areas

FORESTS TODAY

Forested areas

Non-forested areas

Glossary

ALGAL BLOOM – A rapid increase in the amount of algae growing in a body of water. This is usually caused by a change in the light, temperature, flow, or mineral nutrient levels of the water.

ASEXUAL REPRODUCTION – Reproduction without the involvement of gametes or seeds.

ATOMS – The basic particles that make up all substances.

AUXINS – Plant growth hormones. Auxins coordinate many growth and behavioral processes in plants. They can also control other plant hormones.

BIODIVERSITY – The number and variety of different living organisms in a region or environment. Biodiversity also includes the organisms' genetic makeup and the natural communities and ecosystems in which they live.

CHLOROPHYLL – The green pigment found inside chloroplasts in plants. Chlorophyll helps turn energy from the sun into chemical energy during the process of photosynthesis.

COMPENSATION POINT – This is the point at which photosynthesis and respiration are happening at an equal rate within a plant.

COMPOUND – A chemical that is made from two or more elements. An element is a particle that cannot be broken down further without losing its chemical identity, such as an atom of oxygen.

CROSS-POLLINATION – The transfer of pollen from one plant to another. The resulting offspring has a different genetic makeup than its parents.

DECOMPOSE – To be broken down, or to rot or decay, as a result of the action of microorganisms or fungi.

DENATURE – Occurs when the three-dimensional structure of a chemical is changed, usually as a result of heat. The changed chemical—for example, an enzyme—no longer works.

DENITRIFICATION – The loss or removal of nitrogen or nitrogen-containing compounds. Some anaerobic bacteria can carry out this process in soil.

ANSWERS

page 8 Test yourself (top)
(1) A cactus in a dry desert obtains its water either by having very long roots or by having roots spread out in a wide circle close to the surface. In this way, the cactus can tap into deep water stores or is able to catch rainfall as quickly as possible from nearer the surface. The cactus obtains mineral nutrients through its roots from the soil or sand. The leaves allow some gaseous exchange, but spines and a thick outer coating help to preserve water. Cacti in dry deserts have plenty of sunlight.

(2) A water lily on a pond obtains water and mineral nutrients from the pond water. It has small roots, as water is in abundance. Its stem anchors the leaf so that it is on the water surface and faces the sun. It also has a large surface area to collect as much sunlight as possible.

page 8 Test yourself (bottom)
The amount of solution, original size and type of seedling, and the amount of sunlight should be kept the same. These factors should be kept the same so that any results are because of the conditions specific to each experiment. To record changes in the seedlings, the length of each seedling can be measured using a ruler. The number of discolored leaves can be counted and the leaf shape observed.

(1) The plants would be stunted, and the leaf shape would be abnormal.
(2) Seedling growth would be poor.
(3) Seedling growth would be poor, and the leaves would be yellow.
(4) The plants would grow well and look healthy.
(5) The plants would not grow well. They would be stunted, the leaves would be yellow and abnormally shaped, and the roots would not grow properly.

page 11 Investigate
Organic farming uses only natural fertilizers, pesticides, and nutritional supplements. Hormones and synthetic chemicals are not used at all. Nonorganic farming uses synthetic fertilizers, pesticides, and supplements.

page 13 Test yourself
Draining waterlogged soil helps to reduce denitrifying bacteria in the soil, which helps keep the soil nitrogen-rich. Plowing turns over the top layer of the soil, which helps to mix any leftover crop from the previous year into the soil. Plowing also improves oxygen circulation and reduces denitrifying reactions. Using NPK fertilizers adds nutrients directly to the soil, which makes it more fertile. Peas and beans have nitrogen-fixing bacteria in their root nodules, which increases the nitrogen concentration of the soil.

page 21 Investigate
If a plant has successfully carried out photosynthesis, it will contain starch in its leaves. Iodine solution turns

DIFFUSION – Occurs when a substance moves from where it is in high concentration to where it is in low concentration.

ENZYMES – Proteins that help a chemical reaction to take place.

EUTROPHICATION – The accumulation of nutrients, often fertilizers, in a body of water. This results in the excessive growth of organisms and, ultimately, a lack of oxygen in the water.

EVOLUTION – A change in the traits of living organisms over generations.

FERTILIZATION – The fusion of male and female gametes to form a new organism.

FOOD CHAINS – The feeding relationships between species in a group of living organisms. They describe the transfer of material and energy from one species to another within an ecosystem.

GAMETES – The sex cells. These contain half of the genetic information necessary to create a new organism. Pollen grains contain the male gamete, and the ovule contains the female gamete.

GEOTROPISM – A plant's growth movement in response to gravity.

MOLECULES – Two or more atoms joined together. For example, a water molecule is made up of two hydrogen atoms joined together with one oxygen atom.

NITRIFICATION – The chemical process in which nitrogen in plant and animal wastes and dead remains is changed first into nitrites and then into nitrates. This is usually carried out by nitrifying bacteria.

PHOTOSYNTHESIS – The use of sunlight to convert water and carbon dioxide into glucose and oxygen.

PHOTOTROPISM – A plant's growth movement in response to light.

RESPIRATION – The use of oxygen to convert carbohydrates into carbon dioxide and water.

SELF-POLLINATING – Plants in which pollen is transferred from one flower to another on the same plant.

TRANSPIRATION – The process by which water is absorbed through a plant's roots and is evaporated into the atmosphere through its leaves.

blue-black in the presence of starch.

page 23 Test yourself
Leaves are arranged on a plant so that they are exposed to as much sunlight as possible. They are thin, which allows gases to pass easily into and out of the plant.
Cuticle—Prevents water loss, allows sunlight to pass through.
Upper epidermis—Is thin to allow sunlight through.
Palisade layer—Contains chloroplasts and is the main site for photosynthesis.
Spongy layer—Loosely packed cells allow space for gaseous exchange. These cells also store starch produced as a result of photosynthesis.
Lower epidermis—Covered with stomata to control movement of gases and water vapor.

page 26 Test yourself
These experiments use de-starched plants so that we can see when starch is produced solely as a result of the experimental conditions.

If de starched plants were not used, all plants would contain starch at the end of the experiment, and it would be impossible to tell whether or not this was as a result of the experimental conditions.

page 27 Test yourself
Lettuces are grown in tunnels made from clear polyethylene plastic because (1) the plastic acts like glass and keeps the internal temperature warmer than the external temperature, which enhances photosynthesis, (2) it protects them from herbivores, and (3) it protects them from strong winds and frost.

page 32 Investigate
The seedlings first grow toward the window. Auxins diffuse to the shady side of the seedling and cause this side to grow faster. When rotated by 180°, the seedlings straighten and begin to grow in the opposite direction, once more toward the light. The auxins have diffused down the new shady side to cause this growth.

Seedlings still grow in the dark, but growth is straight, as auxins are equally distributed on both sides of the shoot and have not been relocated by the presence of light. The resulting seedlings are spindly and weak, as they have not had light to photosynthesize.

page 35 Test yourself
(1) and (4) are insect-pollinated.
(2) and (3) are wind-pollinated.

page 42 Investigate
(1) Germination will take place because the seeds have access to water, oxygen, and warm temperatures.
(2) No germination will occur because there is no water.
(3) No germination will occur because there is no oxygen in boiled water, and the oil prevents entry of any extra oxygen.
(4) There may be some germination, but only very little, as the temperature is too low.

Index

Page references in italics represent pictures.

PHOTO CREDITS – Cover background image Dr. John Brackenbury/Science Photo Library **Front cover images** (bl) Thomas Dodge/Agstock/Science Photo Library (tr) Peter Hansen/www.istockphoto.com **Back cover image** (inset) Peter Hansen/www.istockphoto.com **p.1** (t) Jim Jurica/www.istockphoto.com (bl) Aleksander Bolbot/www.istockphoto.com (br) Octavio Campos Salles/www.istockphoto.com **p.2** April Chun/www.istockphoto.com **p.3** (t) Dan Bannister/www.istockphoto.com (b) Carrie Winegarden/www.istockphoto.com **p.4** (tr) Melissa Carroll/www.istockphoto.com (tl) Auke Holwerda/www.istockphoto.com (br) Clayton Hansen/www.istockphoto.com **p.5** Ifa-Bilderteam Gmbh/Oxford Scientific **p.6** (bl) Rhett Stansbury/www.istockphoto.com (br) Theo Allofs/zefa/Corbis **p.7** Peter Clark/www.istockphoto.com **p.8** Michael Chen/ www.istockphoto.com **p.9** (t) Martin Gabriel/naturepl.com (b) David Shale/naturepl.com **p.10** (t) Craig Lovell/Agstock/Science Photo Library (b) Clayton Hansen/www.istockphoto.com **p.11** Iain Sarjeant/Oxford Scientific **p.12** (t) Steve Hughes/www.istockphoto.com (mtr) Adam Eisley/www.istockphoto.com (ml) Dr. Jeremy Burgess/Science Photo Library (mbr) Aleksander Bolbot/www.istockphoto.com (bl) David Scharf/Science Photo Library **p.12–13** Tanya Weliky/www.istockphoto.com **p.13** Andrzej Tokarski/www.istockphoto.com (m) Monika Wisniewska/www.istockphoto.com (b) Sean Locke/www.istockphoto.com **p.14** Robert Brook/Science Photo Library **p.16** (t) Igor Karon/www.istockphoto.com (mt) Eugenia Kim/www.istockphoto.com (mb) Craig Walsh/www.istockphoto.com (b) Arthur Kwiatkowski/www.istockphoto.com **p.16–17** Tanya Weliky/www.istockphoto.com **p.17** (t) Steven Allan/www.istockphoto.com (m) Dan Bannister/www.istockphoto.com (b) Aaron Pratt/www.istockphoto.com **p.18** (t) Ian Bracegirdle/www.istockphoto.com (b) Reuters/CORBIS **p.20** Pacific Stock/Ron Dahlquist/Oxford Scientific **p.22** (t) Botanica/Burke/Triolo Productions/Oxford Scientific (mt) Daniel Tero/www.istockphoto.com (mb) Melissa Carroll/www.istockphoto.com (b) volkswag63/www.istockphoto.com **p.24** Carrie Winegarden/www.istockphoto.com **p.25** Ifa-Bilderteam Gmbh/Oxford Scientific **p.27** Vic Aboudara/www.istockphoto.com **p.28** Royalty-Free/Corbis **p.29** (t) April Chun/www.istockphoto.com (b) London Scientific Films/Oxford Scientific **p.31** AravindTeki/www.istockphoto.com **p.32** (t) Suzannah Skelton/www.istockphoto.com (b) Stapleton Collection/Corbis **p.34** Satoshi Kuribayashi/Oxford Scientific **p.35** (t) Merlin Tuttle/Science Photo Library (bl) Willem Dijkstra/www.istockphoto.com (mmt) Ray McKenzie/www.istockphoto.com (mmb) AtWaG/www.istockphoto.com (mr) David M. Albrecht/www.istockphoto.com & Lanica Klein/www.istockphoto.com **p.37** (mr) Gordon Swanson/www.istockphoto.com (b) Nik Wheeler/Corbis **p.38** (t) Claude Nurisany & Marie Perennou/Science Photo Library (b) Auke Holwerda/www.istockphoto.com **p.39** (t) David Schleser/Nature's Images/Science Photo Library (b) Phototake Inc./Dennis Kunkel/Oxford Scientific **p.40** Satoshi Kuribayashi/Oxford Scientific **p.41** (t) BSIP, Cardoso/Science Photo Library B.W. Hoffman/Agstock/Science Photo Library **p.42** Norma Cornes/www.istockphoto.com **p.43** Bob Krist/Corbis **p.44** (r) Adrienne Hart-Davis/Science Photo Library (rb) Octavio Campos Salles/www.istockphoto.com **p.45** Ref. for map D. Bryant, et al., *The Last Frontier Forests: Ecosystems and Economies on the Edge*. Washington, D.C.: World Resources Institute, 1997.